SINGING ROBINS

by Fay Robinson

Lerner Publications Company • Minneapolis

This book is available in two editions:
Library binding by Lerner Publications Company
Soft cover by First Avenue Editions
Divisions of Lerner Publishing Group
241 First Avenue North, Minneapolis, MN 55401 U.S.A.

Website address: www.lernerbooks.com

Words in *italic type* are explained in a glossary
on page 30.

Library of Congress Cataloging-in-Publication Data

Robinson, Fay.
    Singing robins / by Fay Robinson.
        p. cm. — (Pull ahead books)
    Summary: Introduces the physical characteristics,
behavior, habitat, and life cycle of robins.
    ISBN 0–8225–3641–2 (hc: alk. paper)
    ISBN 0–8225–3643–9 (pbk.: alk. paper)
    1. American robin—Juvenile literature. [1. American
robin. 2. Robins.] I. Title. II. Series.
QL696.P288R63 2000
598.8'42—dc21   99–16244

Manufactured in the United States of America
1 2 3 4 5 6 — JR — 05 04 03 02 01 00

Have you seen a bird like this one?

This bird is a robin.

Robins live on mountains and
in valleys, in cities and in towns.

Like all birds, robins have feathers.
Wing feathers help robins fly.

They are
light and
strong,
and they
catch the
wind.

Robins are easy to recognize. Their breasts are brick red.

White lines circle their eyes like little glasses.

Robins sing!
You might have heard their song.

It sounds like "cheer up, cheer up."

Male robins sing a lot in the spring.

Do you
know why?

One reason male robins sing
is so females will notice them!

The singing helps females
choose *mates.*

The male and the female robin
find grass and weeds for a nest.

The female builds the nest.

Then she adds mud. The mud hardens to make the nest firm.

The female robin lines the inside of the nest with soft grass.

Why does she make the inside soft?

She does not want her eggs
to break!

The mother robin lays
three to five eggs.

A robin's eggs are light blue,
like the color of the sky.

They are a little larger than
a big grape.

The mother robin sits on her
eggs to keep them warm.

Keeping eggs warm is called
incubation.

POP!
CRACK!
After 13
or 14 days,

baby robins *hatch* from the eggs.

They have almost no feathers.
Their eyes are closed.

Baby robins open their mouths right away!

The mother and father robin take turns feeding their babies.

The babies
grow fast.
In just two
weeks,

they are
ready to
leave the
nest.
They are
fledglings.

The father
robin takes
care of the
fledglings.

He shows them how to fly.

He shows them how to
find food.

Robins eat earthworms
and insects.

They also eat berries.

By fall, the berries and insects
are almost gone.

What will the robins do to
get food?

Robins *migrate.*
They fly south for the winter.

Food is easier to find where
the weather is warmer.

As the time for their trip comes closer, robins *molt.*

They lose their summer feathers and grow thicker, warmer ones.

Robins gather in
groups called *flocks.*

Young and old, robins fly
to their winter homes.

They come back in the spring,
singing that winter is over.

"Cheer up, cheer up!"

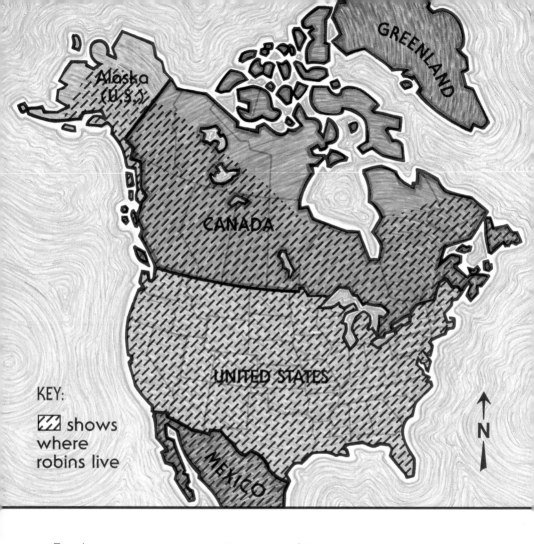

KEY:

☒ shows where robins live

Find your state or province on this map.
Do robins live near you?

Parts of a Robin's Body

head

eye

beak

feather

wing

tail

leg

claw

foot

Glossary

fledglings: baby robins that are ready to leave the nest

flocks: groups of birds that fly together

hatch: come out

incubation: sitting on eggs to warm them so the babies inside will grow

mates: partners for building a nest and raising babies

migrate: to move from one area to another when the seasons change

molt: to lose feathers, which are replaced by new ones

Hunt and Find

The publisher wishes to extend special thanks to our **series consultant,** Sharyn Fenwick. An elementary science-math specialist, Mrs. Fenwick was the recipient of the National Science Teachers Association 1991 Distinguished Teaching Award. In 1992, representing the state of Minnesota at the elementary level, she received the Presidential Award for Excellence in Math and Science Teaching.

About the Author

Fay Robinson has always loved animals and loves to write about them. She is the author of books about creatures such as snakes, lizards, and sloths—even dinosaurs. She also writes books of fantasy. Of the books she has written, her favorite is *Where Did All the Dragons Go?* Fay is a former teacher and a former editor. She lives in Chicago with her dog, Sydney.

Photo Acknowledgments

The photographs in this book are reproduced through the courtesy of: © Alan and Sandy Carey, front cover, pp. 4, 5, 8, 9, 19, 22, 24; © Jennifer Loomis/Animals Animals, back cover; © Barbara Gerlach/Visuals Unlimited (VU), pp. 3, 15; © Rod Planck/Photo Researchers, Inc., p. 6; © Donna Ikenberry/Animals Animals, p. 7; © Richard Day/Daybreak Imagery, pp. 10, 31; © Gregory K. Scott, pp. 11, 18; © Jeffrey Rich Nature Photography, p. 12; © Dwight R. Kuhn, p. 13; © Adam Jones/Photo Researchers, Inc., p. 14; © Michael Habicht/Animals Animals, p. 16; © M. H. Sharp/Photo Researchers, Inc., p. 17; © A. B. Sheldon, p. 20; © Alan and Sandy Carey/Photo Researchers, Inc., p. 21; © S. Maslowski/VU, pp. 23, 26; © Charles Palek/Animals Animals, p. 25; © Vicki J. Anderson/Animals Animals, p. 27.